ADELAIDE

TRAVEL GUIDE

2024-2025

A Journey Through the Heart of South Australia's Coastal Charm

Mabel Martin

TABLE OF CONTENT

MAP OF ADELAIDE

INTRODUCTION

Embarking on a journey to Adelaide was akin to opening a book filled with surprises, a city where every street, every landscape, and every smiling face tells a story. As I pen down this narrative, it's not just an account of travel; it's an invitation to immerse in an experience so profound, that it stays with you long after you've returned home. Adelaide, often overshadowed by its more flamboyant Australian siblings, holds a charm that, once discovered, is irresistible.

My adventure began the moment I set foot in this tranquil city, embraced by the warmth of its people and the serene landscapes that frame it. Adelaide, with its meticulously planned streets, surrounded by lush parklands, whispers stories of its past and present in a rare harmony. It's a city where history coexists with modernity, where the arts flourish, and where nature is revered.

As I wandered through the Adelaide Central Market, the heartbeats of the city were palpable. The air was filled with the aromas of fresh produce, artisan cheeses, and the rich, inviting scent of ground coffee. Each stall was a palette of colors and textures, a testament to the city's diversity and culinary excellence. The market is not just a place for shopping; it's where you experience Adelaide's soul, engaging with locals who are passionate about their produce and proud of their heritage. This interaction was my first brush with the genuine warmth of Adelaidians, setting the tone for the rest of my journey.

The exploration took a more cultured turn as I delved into the city's vibrant arts scene. The Art Gallery of South Australia, with its impressive collection of Australian and Indigenous art, offered a quiet refuge and a feast for the senses. Walking through its halls, I was captivated by stories told through brush strokes and sculptures. It was a profound reminder of the city's rich cultural tapestry and its enduring respect for artistic expression.

Adelaide's commitment to preserving its natural beauty was evident at every turn. The Adelaide Botanic Garden, a verdant oasis amid the urban landscape, was where I found solace and inspiration. The meticulously maintained gardens, with their diverse plant species, were not just a display of botanical beauty but a space where the community comes together to celebrate nature. But Adelaide's narrative wouldn't be complete without mentioning its world-renowned wine regions. A day trip to the Barossa Valley, just a short drive from the city, unfolded like a storybook of vineyards stretching towards the horizon, ancient cellars holding secrets of the winemaking craft, and tastings that were a journey of flavors. The conversations with winemakers, their hands stained with the toil of their craft, their eyes alight with passion for their art, were as intoxicating as the wines they poured. This excursion was not just about wine; it was about connecting with the land and its people, understanding the dedication behind Adelaide's status as a wine capital.

Evenings in Adelaide brought a different kind of magic. The city, illuminated by the soft glow of street lamps, invited strolls along the River Torrens. The sounds of the city at night, the laughter from bustling cafes, and the music from street performers added layers to the city's persona, revealing its youthful, energetic spirit.

As I reflect on my journey, what stands out is not just the beauty of Adelaide or the multitude of experiences it offers. It's the sense of belonging that the city evokes, a testament to its welcoming spirit. Every conversation, every shared meal, and every sunset watching over the ocean at Glenelg Beach felt like a piece of a puzzle that fit perfectly into my own story.

Writing this guide, I want to extend an invitation to you, the reader, to explore Adelaide beyond the pages of this book. It's an encouragement to delve into the city's streets, to engage with its people, and to allow myriad experiences to weave into your narrative. Adelaide is not just a destination; it's a journey of discovery, a place where every traveller can find a piece of themselves among its stories.

This city, with its understated elegance, doesn't clamour for attention but rather, gently invites you to explore its depths. And in doing so, you might just find that Adelaide, with its quiet charm and warm embrace, becomes a part of you, a cherished memory that beckons you back, time and again.

As you turn the pages of this guide, let it be more than an itinerary. Let it be a journey of the heart and soul, a journey that enriches you, leaving footprints not only in the sands of its beaches but also in the corners of your heart. Welcome to Adelaide, where every visit is a story waiting to be told, and every story is an invitation to return.

HISTORY AND CULTURE

South Australia's graceful capital is Adelaide. Unlike other Australian towns like Sydney, Melbourne, and Perth, this chic and laid-back city was not established as a prison colony. Rather, it was a freely established colony of Great Britain from the first. Adelaide's residents continue to take great satisfaction in the fact that their city has never experienced crime.

Culture, art, and legacy

You will experience the spirit of Adelaide's understated elegance and its origins as you journey through its past.

The Kaurna people were the original inhabitants of the Adelaide Plains for tens of thousands of years, living there long before European immigrants came. They took just what they needed for survival and lived in balance with their surroundings. Generation after generation, their culture was based on a profound reverence for the earth, stars, plants, and animals. The spiritual ties to the land that permeates the city's history and culture are still clear examples of their impact.

Adelaide's shoreline, which has several cultural sites important to the Kaurna people and intertwined into their creation tales, is a living testament to its rich indigenous past. In addition, the shoreline has pristine, protected dune ecosystems with abundant biodiversity, underscoring the city's dedication to maintaining its natural beauty.

Apart from its rich past, Adelaide's beaches are also a center for modern art. Large-scale contemporary murals have been painted on the walls all across the area, striking a striking contrast with the industrial and historical settings. These murals revitalize the neighborhood and draw in new tourists by bringing life, light, and color to the urban environment. It's an artistic revolution that combines the city's dynamic current with its rich past in a seamless manner.

The area is also teeming with galleries, artisans, and artists that constitute the vital core of a thriving neighborhood and art scene. The galleries that display the creations of regional artists, these amazing murals, and the many events and exhibits all contribute to the creative vibrancy of the streets. It is possible to fully engage with this vibrant cultural culture, regardless of whether you are an ardent devotee or just someone who values artistic expression.

Adelaide Beaches provides a unique voyage through time and culture, from its ancient foundation to its contemporary creative flourishes. It's a place where culture, art, and community come together to create an experience that honors the region's history while also embracing its dynamic present. You are welcome to join the vibrant narrative of the local art scene, whether you want to participate in it or just stroll about the streets and galleries.

BEST TIME TO VISIT

Adelaide's autumn and spring months, from March to May and September to November, are the finest times to visit. Rainfall is infrequent during these shoulder seasons, and daytime highs are in the 60s and 70s. Moreover, you'll escape the throngs of people and elevated costs linked to the region's busiest time of year, which falls between Adelaide's festival season and the summer vacations. (Note: Due to some high-profile events happening in March, the start of Adelaide's fall, is best avoided if you're looking to grab a discount.) If you're on a budget, visiting Adelaide during the Southern Hemisphere's winter months of June to August is highly recommended, but be prepared for Adelaide's lowest temperatures and more than-average rainfall.

TRANSPORTATION

GETTING TO ADELAIDE CITY

How to Travel to the City from Adelaide Airport

Find the most efficient routes to use to get to the CBD from Adelaide Airport.

The entrance to South Australia is located at Adelaide Airport (ADL). The main airport for the state is about six kilometers from the city center. As soon as you get off the airport, you'll be close to the energetic Rundle Street, the electrifying Adelaide Oval, and the bustling Central Market.

Additionally, if you're searching for the finest methods to go from Adelaide Airport to the City, continue reading to learn how to take an Uber, taxi, or bus.

Bus to the City from Adelaide Airport

Since there are no trains or trams that stop at Adelaide Airport, the simplest method to take public transportation from the airport to the city center is via bus. It takes 25 to 30 minutes to complete the journey, depending on traffic.

The Adelaide Airport to the CBD and back are served by the J1 and J2 buses. During peak hours, an adult one-way ticket costs $4.05 when using MetroCard or Tap and Pay with a debit or credit card that is issued by Visa or Mastercard. During off-peak hours, a one-way bus ticket using the aforementioned payment methods only costs $2.25. During peak hours, the cost of a Singletrip MetroTicket is $5.90 one-way and $4 off-peak.

At Adelaide Airport, the bus stop is situated outside the terminal on the left, right past the taxi rank. Every day, until 11:30 p.m., buses leave Adelaide Airport every 15 to 30 minutes.

The least expensive option for solo travelers to go from Adelaide Airport to the city center is via bus. Be aware that buses may not have enough room for heavy luggage storage, and that this alternative could take a little longer than using a taxi or ridesharing.

Adelaide Airport to City via Taxi

Adelaide Airport's taxi zone is to the left, outside the terminal. It takes somewhat less than 15 minutes and costs around $25 to take a cab from Adelaide Airport to the city center, however, this might change during busy times.

There's no need to reserve a taxi in advance when you arrive at Adelaide Airport; they run on meters.

Taxis are undoubtedly among the fastest methods to go from Adelaide Airport to the city, and they're also reasonably priced whether you're traveling with other people or your bags.

Airport in Adelaide Zone of pickup for ridesharing

There is a designated rideshare pickup area at Adelaide Airport. This implies that you cannot be picked up from the main passenger pickup zone by Uber, Ola, DiDi, or any other ridesharing service if you order one of them.

Rather, go to the left side of the primary pickup area and turn right at the set of lights. Follow the short route, or look for signs leading you to the rideshare pickup location.

PUBLIC TRANSPORTATION

GETTING AROUND ADELAIDE

Adelaide's city center offers free trams and buses, making traveling throughout the area fast and simple.

With so many alternatives for driving, cycling, walking, and public transportation, Adelaide is a very convenient city to navigate. Here's how to navigate Adelaide comfortably.

PORTABILITY IN ADELAIDE

Adelaide has a vast public transportation network that includes trams, trains, and buses. It is advised that you get a MetroCard to use the network. Regular metroCARDs are available for purchase at Adelaide Airport and participating city stores. To discover the closest stop and up-to-date service information, use Adelaide Metro's My Next service feature.

A metroCARD Visitor Pass is also available; for a single, set price, it allows you unrestricted travel on the Adelaide Metro system for three days. The Adelaide Metro InfoCentre, located at the Adelaide Railway Station, is where you can get these cards.

You will need to load your standard metro card with funds to pay for your fares if you pick that option. You may use ticket machines at train stations, participating stores, or MetroCard retail agents to do this.

On trams and O-Bahn busway buses, you may tap and pay with a contactless credit card, debit card, or mobile device. Note that the reduced transfers to other providers are not available with the tap-and-pay option.

When you board the vehicle of your choice, tap your card on the reader to begin your journey.

Adelaide's inner suburbs and city center are serviced by a helpful tram system. It's most practical for getting about the city and to Glenelg, a well-liked beach neighborhood. From 7 a.m. to midnight, the service is offered every 10 to 15 minutes.

In Adelaide's downtown, riders may use the tram for free between South Terrace Station and Entertainment Centre Station.

TRAVELING BY CAR AROUND ADELAIDE

Although driving in Adelaide is simple and safe, you may find that using a mix of public transportation, ridesharing, and taxis is a more convenient way to travel about the city. You may also hire trips to see several breathtaking locations outside of Adelaide, allowing you to delegate the driving.

If you decide to hire a vehicle in the city or at the airport, you may wish to find out whether your hotel has daily parking fees.

There are around 6,000 parking spots spread over nine UPark off-street parking lots run by the City of Adelaide. Using your smartphone, locate parking spots and make contactless payments by downloading the free City of Adelaide Park Adelaide app.

ADDITIONAL TRANSPORTATION MODELS IN ADELAIDE

An excellent way to explore Adelaide is to go on a sightseeing boat around its waterways.

Take a beautiful trip on the riverboat Popeye as it traverses the city center along the River Torrens.

Take a Port River Cruises excursion on the Port Adelaide River to see the dolphins of the Adelaide Dolphin Sanctuary.

CAR RENTALS AND DRIVING TIPS

Numerous automobile rental companies operate throughout Australia, offering a wide range of rental cars in addition to competitive pricing and high-quality services. The primary vehicle rental businesses are:

Hertz, Europcar, Thrifty, AVIS, Judy Budget Access

It's simpler for you to arrive since the majority of these agencies are situated at the airport. If you decide to rent a vehicle later, there are companies located in Adelaide's town center.

Requirements in Adelaide for automobile rentals

To hire and drive a vehicle in Adelaide, or elsewhere in Australia for that matter, you will require:

Possess a valid driver's license and be at least 19 (21 for most employers). If your license is not in English, you could need an international license. Applying for an international driver's license in your hometown before traveling to Australia is the simplest method to get one. You will need to get your driver's license translated by an official NAATI-qualified translator if you do not have an international driver's license.

Possess a credit card for security and payments.

Rental costs

The cost of a car rental in Adelaide varies depending on the company and includes factors like the kind of vehicle and any extras like a rooftop tent or camping gear. The typical cost is usually between $50 and $60 per day, while other organizations have lower weekly or monthly rates. Therefore, hiring a vehicle for a week will run you around $30 a day. Additionally, pricing for reservations made in advance is more appealing than those for last-minute rentals.

For instance:

For a seven-day rental of a compact model

June bookings for pick-up and drop-off at Adelaide (low season)

How to Rent a Car for Less in Adelaide

Reserve the vehicle at least 30 days in advance.

Make use of a price comparison service online.

Visit the offices close to the airport. They have the most competitive pricing.

Get savings if you rent a vehicle for some days.

To avoid any unpleasant surprises in the end, take into account all of the rental terms, including the number of kilometers, the cost of gas, the insurance, and so on.

Split the expenses with other people (in certain cases, the rental fee even includes a second driver).

To avoid paying unanticipated fees, look for a vehicle with few features and low fuel consumption.

The oldest person should drive the automobile if there are multiple of you; the younger the driver, the more expensive it is.

When choosing your reservation dates, keep in mind that costs vary from day to day.

Where in Adelaide should you drive your rental car?

Considered Australia's third biggest island, Kangaroo Island offers a plethora of sights and activities to enjoy. The Flinders Chase National Park, Vivonne Bay, and Kangaroo Island Wildlife Park are three sites that shouldn't be missed.

Barossa Valley: While world-class wine is produced in many South African places, the Barossa Valley is one of the most historically significant and well worth a visit.

Port Lincoln: If you like the outdoors, animals, and unspoiled coastline, Port Lincoln, which is about an hour's flight away by aircraft, is the place for you.

Flinders Ranges: Every traveler should take a trip to the Flinders Ranges because of its breathtaking scenery.

Driving advice for Adelaide

Unless otherwise indicated, the default speed restriction in an urban area is 50 km/h.

Most Australian highways have a 100 kph speed restriction.

Note that there aren't many roads that let you go faster than 110 kph.

At all times, the driver and every passenger in the vehicle must use a seatbelt or child restraint.

Recall that police officers use radar and speed cameras to monitor vehicles traveling at high speeds on all kinds of roadways.

Adelaide parking

Today, the city boasts more parking spots than any other major city—more than the combined amount of Melbourne and Perth—with over 42,000. Please be aware that Adelaide offers both short-term and long-term parking options if you want to drive about the city. Additionally, residents and tourists have a variety of alternatives for enjoying the city thanks to Park'n'Ride services, wheelchair access, and event parking. Find the finest Adelaide Airport parking bargains by browsing our list of car park providers if you're searching for parking close to the airport.

Advice: Since parking signs often change, exercise caution and always verify them before parking.

ACCOMMODATIONS

LUXURY HOTELS AND BOUTIQUE STAYS

The Boutique Hotel Franklin

Founded in 1855 For the traveler who has it all, there is the Franklin Hotel. A little boutique motel upstairs and a lovely tavern below!

Situated in the heart of the city, The Franklin Boutique Hotel Adelaide offers amenities including a restaurant, bar, and complimentary Wi-Fi. Arriving guests are given complimentary pastries in their rooms. A smart TV and a Nespresso coffee maker are provided in every room.

You may find satisfying contemporary Australian meals and pub favorites in the lower kitchen. In addition, the bar offers a selection of drinks that you may sip on the upper balcony, in the beer garden, or anywhere in between.

All of the rooms include contemporary furniture and a refrigerator, and they are all decorated with one-of-a-kind, original artwork by local artists. A bathtub is available in some suites' en suite bathrooms.

The bus station and the Franklin Hotel are across the street from one another. Eight minutes' drive will take you to Rundle Mall for shopping. Adelaide Zoo and the Art Gallery of South Australia are both a 15-minute drive away.

Hotel Mayfair

Luxurious fixtures and amenities with exquisite detailing, excellent and inventive food, exceptional selection, and above all, a guest experience that caters to every need of today's urban wanderer are all integrated.

The opulent Mayfair Hotel, which overlooks Rundle Mall and is centrally located in downtown Adelaide, has a restaurant, lounge bar, and complimentary WiFi. Every room has a 55-inch flat-screen TV and chic décor.

The luxury Adelaide Mayfair Hotel is located 200 meters from the Art Gallery of South Australia, housed in a recently refurbished, heritage-listed structure. Parliament House, Adelaide Oval, and the Adelaide Convention Centre are all three minutes drive away. Airport Adelaide is six km distant.

A hairdryer, tea/coffee-making facilities, and a minibar are included in every air-conditioned room. Every room has a separate bathroom with a shower and complimentary amenities.

The restaurant uses ingredients from the area in its cuisine, while the bar provides a variety of South Australian wines. The property has space for events and meetings.

Hotel Largs Pier

a famous structure with compassion. Sit back on your room's balcony and take in the sunset over the water at this historic hotel. Perfect for a sunny day on the veranda or a wintertime glass of wine by the fireside.

The Largs Pier Hotel offers chic lodging in a structure that is recognized as a historical site. This beachfront home has an on-site restaurant and is just 15 15-minute walk from Semaphore Beach. Certain rooms have balconies with views of the sea.

The South Australian Maritime Museum is ten minutes drive from the Largs Pier Hotel. Driving time to Adelaide City Center is thirty minutes.

There is a flat-screen TV in every room. They have a refrigerator and equipment for preparing tea and coffee. There is a shower, a hair dryer, and complimentary amenities in the private bathroom.

The restaurant serves wood-fired pizza, fish, and hot breakfast to its patrons. Coin-operated laundry facilities and a liquor shop are also available on the premises.

Adelaide Hills' Mount Lofty House & Estate

Situated only fifteen minutes from Adelaide's city center, the renowned Mount Lofty House MGallery is an excellent choice for a hotel and conference getaway.

Renowned English politician and pastoralist Arthur Hardy first constructed Mt. Lofty House as a vacation residence in 1852, needing a break from the Adelaide plains during the summer.

During Arthur Hardy, John Richardson, and Arthur Waterhouse's tenure, the mansion gained notoriety for its lavish dinner parties. The hotel has honored these former proprietors by renaming the Hardys Verandah Restaurant, John Richardson Room, and Arthur Waterhouse Lounge and Bar after them.

All that remained of the property was destroyed by bushfires on Ash Wednesday in January 1983, except for the stone walls. Tragically, the owners had just bought the Mt Lofty House two weeks before and had never moved in. When local Stirling architect Ross Sands bought the House, his goal was to restore it to its former splendor.

The family that now owns it in South Australia is dedicated to maintaining the area's history while also growing Mt. Lofty House to keep it a popular tourist attraction in South Australia.

The Adelaide Hills wine region's Mount Lofty House & Estate Adelaide Hills is housed in a historic rural estate with a view of Piccadilly Valley, yet it's just a 15-minute drive from Adelaide's downtown. A tennis court, croquet grass, and swimming pool are available to visitors. The property is about 450 meters from the viewing point at Mount Lofty Summit.

The magnificently renovated Mount Lofty House & Estate Adelaide Hills - Mount Lofty House & Estate Adelaide Hills is nestled on 18 acres of native gardens and English-style rose gardens. situated close to Mount Lofty Botanic Gardens and Cleland Conservation Park.

There are seven function spaces available for conferences or groups, together with first-rate business and meeting amenities.

The defining dining experience at Mount Lofty House & Estate Adelaide Hills is at the acclaimed Hardy's Verandah Restaurant, which serves a degustation menu that changes periodically.

Day excursions are highly recommended to the adjacent wine country and the historic cities of Hahndorf and Stirling.

BUDGET ACCOMMODATIONS: HOSTELS AND GUESTHOUSES

Budget travel to Adelaide doesn't have to mean sacrificing location or comfort. The city has a range of affordable hostels and guesthouses that combine a friendly vibe with cost to make sure your stay is both affordable and pleasurable.

1. YHA Adelaide Central

Location: This hostel is well located in the center of Adelaide's business district, close to both the lively Rundle Mall and Central Market.

Cost: The starting price for a shared dorm room is around $30 per night.

Overview: Adelaide Central YHA is distinguished by its spotless, cozy lodgings and extensive range of facilities, such as a fully furnished kitchen, a large lounge, and free Wi-Fi. For tourists who want to socialize in a welcoming setting and meet new people, it's ideal. To accommodate a range of tastes and price points, the hostel also provides a selection of accommodation options, including private rooms and shared dormitories.

2. Backpack Oz

Situated on Wakefield Street, it's conveniently close to the Adelaide Botanic Garden and the South Australian Museum, two of the city's main attractions.

Cost: Private rooms are offered at a premium price, with dorm beds starting at around $25 per night.

Overview: Backpack Oz is renowned for its welcoming ambiance and first-rate amenities, which include a bar where visitors may relax and mingle. The guesthouse offers excellent value for money, free breakfast, Wi-Fi, and Tuesday BBQ evenings. To discover Adelaide, Backpack Oz provides a cozy and interesting base, whether you're traveling alone or with the company.

3. Cannon Street Backpackers

Location: This hostel is between the busy East End sector and the Himeji Garden, nestled in the peaceful, green alleys of Adelaide's east end.

Price: A shared room costs $28 per night.

Overview: Perfect for those looking for a peaceful getaway after a day of exploring, this modest, intimate hostel has a homey environment. Guests get access to a living space, free Wi-Fi, and a community kitchen, providing all they need for a peaceful stay. A customized experience is the priority at Cannon Street Backpackers, making it ideal for visitors who value a sense of community.

4. Glenelg Beach Hostel Location: About a 20-minute tram ride from the city center, this hostel is situated in the coastal district of Glenelg, for those who want to stay by the sea.

Cost: Private rooms are available at an additional fee, with dorm accommodations starting at $27 per night.

Overview: Glenelg Beach Hostel offers the best of both worlds, combining the laid-back beach vibe with convenient proximity to Adelaide's attractions. A bar, a shared kitchen, a comfortable lounge area, and beach volleyball are among the amenities. For tourists who want to take advantage of Adelaide's seaside appeal without going over budget, it's the perfect option.

UNIQUE ACCOMMODATIONS: ECO-LODGES AND BEACHFRONT VILLAS

Wilderness Retreat EcoCaddy

Location: Tucked away in the verdant Adelaide Hills, this resort offers a peaceful respite from the city at only a minute's drive.

Cost: Depending on the time of year and kind of lodging, prices start at $200 per night.

Overview: EcoCaddy Wilderness Retreat is a model of environmentally conscious luxury, providing exquisitely built lodges that maximize comfort while minimizing their negative effects on the environment. The resort collects rainwater, grows organic vegetables in its gardens, and runs on sustainable energy. Visitors may take advantage of careful, sustainable environment restoration opportunities, animal observation, and guided nature hikes. Every lodge is designed to provide seclusion and amazing views of the surrounding landscape, making it the ideal option for anybody wishing to relax and experience eco-luxury.

Seascape Lodge situated on Emu Bay

Location: Located on Kangaroo Island's tranquil Emu Bay, a picturesque boat trip from Adelaide.

Cost: Gourmet meals made using regional ingredients are included in the $250 per nightly fee.

Description: With just three opulent guest rooms, Seascape Lodge on Emu Bay is a private beachside retreat and a serene hideaway. The resort is well-known for its sweeping views of the ocean, easy access to the beach, and attentive service. Kangaroo Island's natural beauty, fine dining experiences with locally produced ingredients, and wildlife trips are all available to guests. For those looking for a tranquil getaway with the extra luxury of visiting one of Australia's most stunning islands, this lodge is perfect.

3. Beachfront Villas Adelaide

Location: Just a short drive from Adelaide's downtown are these villas, which are situated in the lively coastal district of Henley Beach.

Cost: A two-bedroom villa starts at $300 per night.

Overview: With direct beach access, contemporary conveniences, and roomy living spaces, Adelaide

Beachfront Villas are the pinnacle of seaside luxury. With big windows and outdoor areas that let visitors take in the breathtaking vistas and sounds of the sea, the villas are intended to make the most of their gorgeous beachfront setting. These villas provide the ideal location for leisure and creating memories by the beach, whether you're planning a family holiday or a romantic retreat.

EXPLORING ADELAIDE'S CITY CENTER

RUNDLE MALL

The best place to shop in South Australia is Rundle Mall, which is home to some of the most prestigious flagship shops in the state, such as Sephora, Tiffany & Co., and H&M. In the center of Adelaide, sandwiched between the trendy East End and the energetic West End, lies the family-friendly Rundle Mall, a year-round center of activity and excitement.

Rundle Mall has everything for everyone with over 700 retail shops, 300 services, 3 department stores, 15 arcades and entertainment centers, as well as restaurants and eating establishments. Between Pulteney Street and King William Street is an outdoor mall. Grenfell Street borders the southern side, while the buildings on the northern side back onto North Terrace.

Rundle Mall entertains 22 million people a year with a variety of high-profile events, such as the Tasting Australia, Adelaide Fringe Festival, and Vogue Festival, in addition to activations, pop-ups, and a wide array of internationally renowned buskers.

There's usually something going on at Gawler Place Canopy, particularly on weekends and during school breaks.

Landmarks

Award-winning artwork may be seen throughout The Mall, such as the well-known piece The Spheres by Bert Flugelman, sometimes referred to as the "Mall's Balls," "Pigeon" by Paul Sloan, and "A Day Out" by Marguerite Derricourt, which includes the well-known bronze pigs Horatio, Oliver, Truffles, and Augusta.

Past Events

Originally, Rundle Street was extended to become Rundle Mall. In November 1972, then-Premier Don Dunstan declared that a portion of Rundle Street would be closed. Ian Hannaford Architects was given the task of removing the road and replacing it with asphalt.

Rundle Mall debuted as a car-free retail area on September 1, 1976. Ten thousand people flocked to celebrate the start of a new era in city shopping when

Don Dunstan arrived by horse and cart and champagne flowed through the fountain.

Hours of Operation: Rundle Mall is open almost all year round, seven days a week. While some establishments are open outside of these hours, the majority of stores are open during these hours. For precise details, please refer to the listings for each shop.

In the City, Friday means late-night shopping.

Weekdays: 9 a.m. to 5.30 p.m.

Friday: 9 a.m. to 9 p.m.

Saturday: 9 a.m.–5 p.m.

Sunday: 11 a.m. to 5 p.m.

Public Holidays: 11 a.m. to 5 p.m. (may vary)

CULTURAL ATTRACTIONS: MUSEUMS, GALLERIES AND THEATERS

Adelaide is a creative metropolis. Amazing outdoor murals, fascinating museums, and fantastic festivals contribute to a vibrant art and cultural environment. Examine a selection of Adelaide's must-see theaters, museums, and art galleries to add to your schedule.

SOUTH AUSTRALIAN MUSEUM

Where: North Terrace

The best natural history museum in the city is the South Australian Museum. Discover fossil collections, Aboriginal item exhibitions, and expedition tales from the Antarctic. Youngsters will like the digital adventure game Shadow Initiation, which requires you to solve riddles and discover the museum's mysteries.

Southeastern Australia's art gallery

Where: North Terrace

The Art Gallery of South Australia, which has one of the best art collections in Australia, is breathtaking on the inside as well as the outside. Through its imposing pillars on North Terrace, enter to peruse over 45,000 pieces spanning two millennia. There's always a surprise around the corner at the gallery since it features a variety of media, from paintings to metalwork.

ACE OPEN

Where: North Terrace

ACE Open, one of the most captivating contemporary art galleries in the city, strives to be both friendly and challenging. You should anticipate your thoughts to be changed and your preconceptions to be questioned since the ACE Open is a location where artists and audiences may take chances. Check out what's on; the gallery's shows change often.

TANDANYA

Location: City Center

Tandanya is a gallery not to be missed, showcasing the cultural expressions of artists who are Aboriginal and Torres Strait Islander. The gallery is called after the Kaurna phrase for "place of the red kangaroo," and it is situated on Kaurna (pronounced "Garna") property. In addition to amazing visual art pieces, Tandanya features live music acts and performing arts events.

JAMFACTORY

Location: West End

JamFactory, which is situated in Adelaide's hip West End creative district, is dedicated to valuing art and design. The gallery has an exhibition area that features a variety of collectable crafts and designs in addition to four workshops dedicated to metal, glass, furniture, and ceramics. Take in a glassblowing demonstration before exploring the displays.

ADELAIDE STREET ARTS

Where: Adelaide and its environs

Not all of South Australia's most intriguing artwork is seen in museums; some may be found painted in alleyways, on street corners, and even on large grain silos. Adelaide's street art exhibits a wide variety of creative expression, from intricate portraiture to classic graffiti. See some of the greatest outdoor art in the city by following the Adelaide Street Art Trail. Huge murals painted atop grain silos and water towers along the Australian Silo Art Trail are a rewarding side excursion from the city.

MOD

Where: The heart of Adelaide

MOD is a museum that occupies a space halfway between science and art. MOD is a future science and technology display space at the University of South Australia, where visitors may investigate, learn, and be inspired by how these fields are shaping our view of the world. Although the museum's displays are intended for visitors who are at least 15 years old, all ages are welcome.

NATIONAL MUSEUM OF RAILWAYS

Where: Adelaide's Port

The National Railway Museum is Australia's biggest underground railway museum, perfect for history and train enthusiasts. There are more than 100 displays here that teach you about Australia's railway history. Take in the sight of massive steam engines, stroll through exquisite train carriages, and even take a train trip.

ADELAIDE MUSIC CENTER

Where: Central Business District

The Adelaide Festival Centre, sometimes referred to as the "heart of the arts" in Adelaide, is the leading venue for theater, dance, music, and exhibits in the city. The venue's busy schedule offers something for everyone; consider jazz evenings, vintage operas, and family-friendly shows. In addition, the theater spaces are astounding; the Festival Theatre has three floors with seating for about 2,000 people.

GREEN SPACES: ADELAIDE BOTANIC GARDEN AND RIVER TORRENS

Charm and splendor of the Botanic Garden in Adelaide

North Terrace, Adelaide Botanic Garden, Adelaide, SA 5000

Without a doubt, one of Australia's most beautiful cities is Adelaide. Adelaide certainly has a lot to offer the sight, from the luxuriant parklands that run down the River Torrens to the many elaborate cathedrals scattered across the city center to the immaculate Glenelg Beach!

This in turn implies that The Festival City has an excellent botanic garden. The Adelaide Botanic Garden is an amazing jumble of exquisite gardens, cutting-edge architecture, and wide boulevards, all accompanied by an abundance of educational opportunities.

So what is it about this bustling metropolis that makes the Adelaide Botanic Garden such a serene destination? exquisitely planned gardens

Each of the opulent, colorful gardens that make up the Adelaide Botanic Garden showcases the marvels of Australian flora and animals. First Creek Wetland is the park's main water supply in addition to being a lovely section of the landscape. Its crucial, breathtaking beauty cannot be overstated.

The incredible Garden of Health is another example of how plants may enhance human health and wellness. This significant garden demonstrates how plants and flowers may have therapeutic qualities that modern medicine is unable to supply by skillfully fusing Western and non-Western civilizations.

Last but not least, don't miss seeing the International Rose Garden, a charming section of the botanic garden that has over 5,000 roses—how sweet!

The era of space Centennial Conservatory

The Bicentennial Conservatory, a massive, curved monument to the world's tropical rainforests, is an amazing work of design in and of itself. Before entering the conservatory, where plants from Australia, Papua New Guinea, Indonesia, and the rainforests of the Pacific Islands await you, take some time to admire the steel and glass edifice itself.

The incredible Garden of Health is another example of how plants may enhance human health and wellness.

This significant garden demonstrates how plants and flowers may have therapeutic qualities that modern medicine is unable to supply by skillfully fusing Western and non-Western civilizations.

Last but not least, don't miss seeing the International Rose Garden, a charming section of the botanic garden that has over 5,000 roses—how sweet!

The era of space Centennial Conservatory

The Bicentennial Conservatory, a massive, curved monument to the world's tropical rainforests, is an amazing work of design in and of itself. Before entering the conservatory, where plants from Australia, Papua New Guinea, Indonesia, and the rainforests of the Pacific Islands await you, take some time to admire the steel and glass edifice itself.

The Santos Economic Botany Museum

With more than 130 years of existence, the Santos Museum of Economic Botany is a joyful tribute to plants and the last of its type. It's almost like walking into a delightful plant time capsule since this permanent plant collection is almost the same as the initial exhibit that debuted all those years ago!

Have a relaxing day in the garden.

Everyone enjoys the Adelaide Botanic Garden, which is a charming and serene area of the city. The Adelaide Botanic Garden is a fantastic day trip destination for anybody visiting the city, whether they want to explore the tastefully designed gardens, learn about ancient rainforests, or just enjoy the sight of century-old flora.

RIVER TORRENS

From its source in the Adelaide Hills at Mount Pleasant, the River Torrens travels 85 km over the Adelaide Plains, past the Adelaide city center, and empties into Gulf St. Vincent via a man-made outlet between Henley Beach South and West Beach. It forms the Torrens Lake between the Adelaide Zoo and a weir across from Adelaide Gaol as it travels between the city center and North Adelaide.

The River Torrens is often referred to as the 'river of the Red Gum forest', or Karra wirra-parry, by the indigenous Kaurna people. It speaks of the thick forest of eucalyptus trees that bordered its banks until the first settlers cleared them.

Many seasonal streams that are dry for most of the year feed the River Torrens. The flow of the Torrens and its tributaries may vary greatly; at times it can be a roaring torrent that destroys bridges and floods metropolitan areas, or it might trickle and dry up in the summer. The Torrens have often flooded since colonization, sometimes with tragic results.

The river flows through the heart of Adelaide, therefore building several bridges was necessary for transportation. Floods destroyed the majority of the early timber-built bridges, prompting the construction of new ones.

There are several playgrounds, footpaths, and bike paths throughout the 35 km of park that runs beside the River Torrens. Plants native to the area have been replanted as parks around the river have been built. The river has drawn many tourists ever since European settlers arrived. The river is often utilized for leisure, with runners and bikers frequently using the riverfront trails. The lake is used all year round by rowers for training, and the summer months see some regattas hosted on the Torrens Lake circuit.

A focal point of many Adelaide events and picture-perfect landscapes is Torrens Lake. Elder Park, which bears Sir Thomas Elder Smith's name, is an iron rotunda bandstand dating from 1882 that was mostly constructed in Glasgow and located on the south side of the lake next to the Adelaide Festival Centre. Elder Park is also the site of various yearly public events, such as the Tasting Australia festival and the annual "Carols by Candlelight" event, which features a mass singing of Christmas carols.

With movies, live music, food, and wine available on the Riverbank, the Adelaide Pontoon on the River Torrens has been revitalized as the Recreational ferries known as "Popeye" boats are privately owned and run on the lake between Elder Park and the Adelaide Zoo. In March 1977, Popeye 5's ferrying of Queen Elizabeth II and Prince Philip, followed by a choir in Popeye 4, gave the Popeyes their first taste of royalty. In 1982, the wooden Popeyes I, II, and III were swapped out.

Long-necked tortoises thrive on the steep riverbanks in some areas. Around 100 different kinds of native waterfowl may be spotted along the river, including Pacific black ducks, Australian wood ducks, black swans, ibis, egrets, and herons. The riverbanks are home to river red gum and blue gum trees. Sheoak, native cherry, native pine, and golden wattle Australia's floral emblem are also found there.

FOOD AND WINE

TOP RESTAURANTS

In recent years, Adelaide's cuisine culture has flourished. It seems like there are new places to go and activities to try every week. Look no further than Adelaide's amazing choice of restaurants whether you're searching for something sweet or a new eatery that mixes exquisite cuisine with a contemporary edge. Adelaide's stunning natural features and top-notch entertainment make it the perfect spot to sample things to come.

Hains & Co.'s

House-made sausage buns, along with black pepper, Shiraz, and tomato chutney, are their best-known offering for sea pigs.

CONCERNING HAINS & CO

Wander through obscure passageways in the western part of the city to find Hains & Co., Adelaide's renowned cocktail and gin bar, located on Gilbert Place. This popular place, which has a fondness for whiskey and cigars, also has a distinctive patio that is perfect for fostering wonderful conversations over delicious libations and bar bites. You wouldn't believe this is a CBD location. With its hanging greenery, gently shimmering pendant lights, and polished wood, the place exudes an eclectic ambiance that is perfect for pre-dinner cocktails or after-work catchups. You may want to order the popular Yuzu Fancy cocktail, which is made with gin, sweet flowers, mandarin, lemon juice, and yuzu liqueur. Raise a glass of gin laced with jalapeños and serve it with appetizers such as golden fried halloumi, accompanied by generous portions of lemon, honey, and thyme.

5000 SA, 23 Gilbert Place, Adelaide CBD

Garcon Bleu

Chateaubriand is best known for two: SA Beef Angus 100% grass-fed, pommes Anna, carrots with a honey glaze, and béarnaise sauce.

Concerning Garcon Bleu

Discover Adelaide's newest culinary destination, Garcon Blue, on Currie Street in the city center. It offers a contemporary take on the "new French" idea. This sophisticated restaurant, which is tucked away in the

Sofitel Adelaide, radiates sophistication with its polished wood, dramatic lighting, and luxurious blue velvet seating—perfect for a romantic get-together or post-work cocktails with friends. Anticipate a straightforward, avant-garde experience that is best savored while sipping excellent wine and engaging in stimulating conversation. Start your unforgettable gastronomic journey with venison tartare, slow-cooked egg and beetroot, or marron, bisque, rouille, and Warrigal greens. For the main course, consider sharing a seafood symphony that includes lamb shoulder and white bean cassoulet, or grilled Southern rock lobster, SA King prawns, squid, mussels, clams, and Smoky Bay oysters.

Adelaide CBD, SA's 108 Currie Street

Fish Out of Water Hyde Park is most known for
The greatest burgers in town are served with fresh, regional seafood.
CONCERNING FISH OUT OF HYDE PARK WATER
At Adelaide's Fish Out of Water on King William Road in Hyde Park, enjoy delicious seafood. At this lively

restaurant, where crimson stools, blue leather banquette seats, and cozy tables are tucked beneath an octopus mural while mouthwatering smells come from the kitchen, fish and chips is the epitome of pleasure. The best-tasting cuisine starts with fresh ingredients. Consider fish like salmon, barramundi, and King George whiting that may be fried, crumbed, or char-grilled to your preference, along with a variety of delectable housemade salads and crispy chips. Or have a portion of the fisherman's basket, which includes crumbed butterfish, scallops, prawns, calamari, chips, and tartar sauce. Another option is to indulge in a marinated lamb burger with cheese, eggplant, tomatoes, capsicum, olives, lettuce, and sweet chili sauce.

Hyde Park, South Africa 117 King William Road

The best known for its contemporary take on quality Italian cuisine is Luciano's Italian Marina Pier.

Concerning the Italian Riviera of Luciano

Luciano's Italian Marina Pier at Holdfast Shore Marina in Glenelg serves Italian cuisine with a touch of the Amalfi Coast. This tastefully designed restaurant is all class with tiled flooring, sandstone walls, and gently lighting downlights, making it the perfect setting for romantic evenings with that special someone. It has the best waterfront views from the marina pier. A well-stocked bar is available for those looking for a post-work drink, and an open kitchen allows patrons to see chefs in action.

Alternatively, have a slow-roasted wrapped pork belly with fennel cream, kipfler chips, watercress, and nduja butter.

Holdfast Shores Marina, Shops 13–15 Marina Pier, Glenelg, SA

The best-known dish at Cafe di Roma is fettuccine with red wine Napoli sauce, slow-cooked lamb ragu, leeks, carrots, and celery.

CONCERNING CAFE DI ROMA

Café di Roma on Prospect Road offers hospitable Italian hospitality that is both warm and inviting. With its bright decor of red tablecloths, polished wood flooring, and walls of maroon and olive green, this Adelaide restaurant has been serving the community for many years. It's the perfect place to unwind with friends over a fragrant cup of coffee. Enjoy a meal outside on red lattice seats during warm weather while reflecting on a genuine, lovingly prepared cuisine. You may even grab a piece of Al Mondo pizza, which has mozzarella, smoked leg ham, Italian salami, roasted capsicum, pineapple, spring onions, mushrooms, and olives. Pasta fans may have fettuccine with chunks of chicken breast, basil, tomato, and avocado in a thick, creamy sauce; or try the veal or chicken parmigiana, which comes with salad and chips and is topped with ham, mozzarella, and Napoli sauce.

Prospect SA, 116A Prospect Road

BAROSSA VALLEY AND MCLAREN VALE: WINE-TASTING TOURS

This deluxe trip provides a close-up look at Australia's wine region, the Barossa Valley. It's a full-day excursion that highlights the best wines and gourmet food that the area has to offer.

Features: Guests may try a variety of varietals, including the well-known Barossa Shiraz, during the tour's visits to famous vineyards. In addition to tastings, a gourmet lunch at a nearby vineyard enhances the experience by providing meals that ideally pair with the wines. This trip is ideal for anyone who wants to learn more about wine in an area that is well-known across the world. Skilled experts provide insights into the history, terroir, and winemaking process.

Cost: From $250 per person, which covers transportation from Adelaide, lunch, and all tastings.

Overview of the McLaren Vale Explorer Tour: Renowned for its Mediterranean climate and sustainable winemaking practices, McLaren Vale produces outstanding Cabernet, Grenache, and Shiraz. The

Explorer Tour takes visitors on an exploration of the area's hidden treasures and small vineyards.

Features: This full-day trip offers visits to many renowned vineyards where participants may learn about organic and biodynamic winemaking techniques. It is both gorgeous and instructive. A delicious lunch at a nearby winery with the fresh, regional cuisine of McLaren Vale is part of the experience. The opportunity to interact with the winemakers will be appreciated by wine lovers as it offers a personal touch and insights into their creative process.

Cost: All wine tastings, lunch, and round-trip transportation from Adelaide are included in the starting price of around $220 per person.

Overview of the Barossa Valley and McLaren Vale Wine Tour: Icons of South AustraliaWith this trip, visitors may experience the best of both worlds if they can't pick between McLaren Vale and the Barossa Valley. This all-encompassing two-day excursion showcases the variety of South Australia's wine landscape by visiting the most well-known wineries in both areas.

Features: Tastings at upscale wineries in both areas, overnight lodging in the Barossa Valley, and exclusive access to facilities used for wine production behind closed doors are all included in the trip. Gourmet dining experiences reflecting regional delicacies will be provided to guests, along with skillfully chosen wine pairings for their meals. This trip offers a fantastic chance to have an extensive wine education while discovering the breathtaking scenery and award-winning cuisine of South Australia's most prestigious wine districts.

Cost: From $500 per person, you may enjoy an all-inclusive wine country immersion that includes all tastings, meals, lodging, and transportation.

LOCAL MARKETS

There's a market in Adelaide that suits your requirements, whether you're looking for antique jewels, fresh fruit, or vintage finds.

Stirling Marketplace, Stirling

Visit the Stirling Market in the Adelaide Hills once a month, generally in the second half, from 10 a.m. to 4 p.m. Stroll down the street lined with artisan booths to discover a variety of items such as apparel, plants, jewelry, dried fruit, pottery, olive oil, and crafts. Take in the fresh air and live music while you shop. In addition to the abundant and delicious cuisine that is constantly available, Stirling is a summertime hotspot, an autumnal celebration, a cozy winter setting, and an amazing springtime destination.

Where: Stirling's Druid Avenue

Adelaide's Gathered Design Market

The Gathered Design Market is held periodically in the city's Torrens Parade Ground from 10 a.m. to 4 p.m. A carefully chosen selection of regional producers and designers may be found in the marketplace. Consider things like apparel, accessories, jewelry, luggage, candles, skincare products, pottery, and makeup, to mention a few. And what would a market stroll be without stopping for lunch or brunch? Sweets and savory treats are always available, along with gin, juice, and coffee for a quick energy boost in the morning.

Where: Adelaide's Torrens Parade Ground

Adelaide Showground Farmers' Market, Wayville

Adelaide's newest spot to browse is Market In The Mall, a monthly Sunday market held under Rundle Mall's Gawler spot Canopy from 9 am to 5 pm. It is organized by the same team that brings you the seasonal Gathered Market. Like the seasonal Gathered Market, the new market has carefully chosen products from local producers and designers, including clothes, home items, art, jewelry, purses, candles, pottery, skincare, and cosmetics, to mention a few. There will be gozleme, filled arepas, and donuts available for brunch and lunch, along with wine, gin, and juices.

Where: Rundle Mall's Gawler Place Canopy

Wayville's Adelaide Showground Farmers' Market

Every Sunday from 8:30 a.m. to 12 p.m., the very charming Adelaide Showground Farmers' Market is hosted. The greatest seasonal products and market treats from nearby stallholders may be found here. Rain or shine, it's a great way to start the day and a foodies' paradise! In addition to the farm-fresh fruits and vegetables, the handmade food prepared by the local chefs will warm your spirit from the inside out.

Where: Adelaide Showground, Wayville, Rose Terrace

Gilles at Wayville's Grounds

Every month, Gilles At The Grounds brings life to the old Brick Dairy at the Wayville Showgrounds, running from a sharp 9 a.m. to 3 p.m. More than 100 market booths provide everything you could want for your shopping requirements, including eco-friendly items, retro home goods, and clothing. Delectable food options include plant-based lamb yiros and exquisite cupcakes, and there's live music from local singers. Your dog is also quite welcome.

Where: Adelaide Showgrounds Brick Dairy, South Boulevard (access via Leader Street gate)

Adelaide's Central Market

The Adelaide Central Market, perhaps the largest and greatest in Adelaide, is top-notch and has an abundance of delicious cuisine. Having first opened its doors in 1869, the gourmet grounds now include over 80 booths, making it one of the Southern Hemisphere's biggest hidden fresh produce markets. You may find plenty of locally grown fruit, flowers, health stores, bakeries and patisseries, artisan cheeses, continental meats, and more along the colorful interior lanes. In addition, there's a diverse range of restaurants, both new and old, taverns, culinary classes, and live music.

Where: Adelaide, 44–60 Gouger St.

BEACHES AND COASTAL ATTRACTIONS

GLENELG BEACH: ACTIVITIES AND FAMILY FUN

The Kaurna people inhabited the Adelaide Plains and resided in Glenelg before 1936.

The Buffalo (together with four other ships) then made landfall at Glenelg, carrying the first British immigrants to the recently established colony of South Australia.

After making their first halt at Kingscote on Kangaroo Island, they continued after discovering that there was no fresh water to be discovered. Holdfast Bay got its name from the fact that its anchors "held fast" in this area, keeping the ships stable.

Governor Sir John Hindmarsh named the colony the "Colony of South Australia" on December 28, 1836. He was standing at what is now known as the Old Gum Tree in Glenelg (see below).

The port was eventually relocated to the more advantageous site that is now Port Adelaide, and the settlement's center quickly shifted inland, although Glenelg kept developing into a thriving town.

Glenelg turned into an affluent person's playground in the early 1900s. Mansions were springing up everywhere, and people liked to hang out along the Glenelg Pier.

Luna Park, identical to the one that remains today in St Kilda, Melbourne, was located next to the pier. This amusement park was eventually taken down and served as the foundation for the most famous Luna Park ever, which is located in Sydney Harbor.

Nowadays, Glenelg is a well-liked vacation spot for both tourists and residents. It provides a crowded dining area with plenty of eateries, pubs, and entertainment options.

While Glenelg is a fantastic location all year round, summer is when it truly shines (as with other beach towns!).

Directions to Glenelg

Situated on a beach, Glenelg is around 11 kilometers southwest of Adelaide's city center. Straight along the Anzac Highway is a simple journey that takes around twenty minutes on average.

Taking the tram is the most convenient method to go to Glenelg on public transportation. Tickets for a single adult are presently $6.20, and it runs about every twenty minutes.

Concession and kid-friendly tickets are offered, and using a MetroCard also results in a discount. Visit the Adelaide Metro website to discover all the additional costs.

Activities in Glenelg

Even if you don't have a plan for the day, Glenelg is the place to go if you're stuck in Adelaide with nothing to do. Go to "The Bay," as the locals like to refer to it, and take a stroll along Jetty Road.

Take a stroll down the jetty, have lunch at a café or restaurant, peruse the stores, and get an ice cream. See a film in the afternoon and have a beverage at one of the numerous pubs as the sun sets.

In Glenelg, there are also many free activities available.

However, I've included this list in case you need to know about the Glenelg attractions.

Shop Until You Drop

Boutiques may be found all along Jetty Road and sometimes even on the smaller side streets. Shopping at Glenelg will feel more like it did in the past than it does at the large malls.

Here, you won't only see the same old names; instead, you'll discover unusual home goods, adorable clothes, and some excellent presents at smaller, local shops.

Every time I visit Piper Homewares and Denim & Cloth (on Waterloo St.), I like to pick up some chocolate from Haighs!

Take a ride on the Ferris wheel

The Skyline Ferris Wheel in Glenelg is packed up and put into hibernation for the winter, so it is only open during the summer.

It appears every year in October as the Mix102.3 Giant Wheel and remains there until May. It provides daily views from 10 am to 9:30 pm of Glenelg, the beach, and the surrounding suburbs.

Treat yourself to a cocktail at Moseley Beach Club.

Even though we won't be able to go to one of Bali's well-known beach clubs this summer, we can nevertheless experience similar vibes right here at Glenelg Beach. Among the top tourist destinations in Glenelg is this one!

In 2017, the Moseley Beach Club made its debut on the beach somewhat to the north of the Glenelg jetty. It's becoming a welcomed and well-liked summertime attraction.

This was Australia's first beach club in a European manner, and it marked the beginning of a trend that has since expanded across the state and to other beaches in South Australia.

Keep an eye out for the unique touches this summer as the theme for this year's celebration of all things Greek, Greece, is 23/24 summer.

Although it costs nothing to enter the Moseley Beach Club, renting a daybed or a lounger is an additional expense.

They have an extensive menu with lots of food to sustain you, along with a variety of beverages, including a cocktail in a pineapple that you just must post on Instagram. A modest kids' menu is also available.

They open early on weekends for breakfast, and DJs often play records later throughout the day.

Bring the children to The Beach House

One of the finest things to do in Glenelg with kids is to visit The Beachouse, a family amusement park that is located directly on the beach.

Kids will enjoy coming here to play mini golf, ride the dodgem cars and bumper boats, and slide down the waterslides, among many other activities!

The Beachouse does not charge admission; instead, you pay for what you use. Nonetheless, there will often be timed times when a single purchase covers everything. Especially on the weekends and during school breaks, keep an eye out for them in the mornings.

Children will like the unpaid play area.

Young children will adore this fantastic free playground located just on the seafront between the Beachouse and the jetty. This is the spot to stop when your kids need to let off some steam, even if you are simply walking down the street.

At ground level, there are little trampolines and climbing obstacles.

The youngsters will enjoy playing in the water feature in neighboring Moseley Square if the weather is warm. They love to run through the jets that shoot up from the ground to cool down. Adults may even want to join them!

Eat Yourself Silly

Glenelg has an enormous selection of dining alternatives. You can find whatever you may desire here, at some point. Everything is available here, including chain restaurants and quick food, cafés and takeout, pub meals and fine dining.

The eateries are dispersed across the area.

Consider the Glenelg Marina Pier for alternatives like Sammy's on the Marina and the Marina Sunset Bar if you're searching for a bit fancier dining.

Around Jetty Road are fast-food restaurants, cafés, and more laid-back locations.

For decent pub grub, I suggest Doughballs Pizza; for coffee and dessert, try St. Louis House of Fine Ice Cream & Dessert; and for pub grub, try Moseley Bar and Restaurant.

Enroll in a Photography Class

If you're searching for something to do at night in Glenelg, how about this? Adventure Art Photography will teach you night photography as you spend a fun evening at the beach.

You will learn the finest techniques for shooting gorgeous sunsets and long-exposure water photographs that are often seen hanging on walls during the three-hour course.

In addition to learning how to snap the ideal nighttime picture, you'll attempt light painting the Ferris wheel for some fun.

That would make a wonderful memento from your trip to Glenelg!

Consume ice cream.

I realize I've already included some restaurants, but I wanted to bring up ice cream in particular. After all, getting ice cream at the beach is almost a must.

There are a ton of ice cream businesses in Glenelg, ranging from the sit-down café St. Louis House of Fine Ice Cream & Dessert to all the typical hole-in-the-wall establishments like Copenhagen, Gelatissimo, and Cold Rock.

My particular favorite, however, is the recently opened Bottega Gelateria on Jetty Road, which serves a variety of delectable pastries, some of which are plant-based.

HENLEY BEACH: DINING AND SUNSETS

Henley Beach, a stunning coastal jewel in Adelaide, provides a tranquil haven with its immaculate beaches, glistening waves, and lively local scene. This beach is a location where leisure, adventure, and gastronomic pleasures come together, offering the ideal setting for both exploration and relaxation. It's not simply a place to soak up the sun. Here's a closer look at Henley Beach, which is a must-visit location in Adelaide due to its abundance of activities, food options, and famous sunsets.

Amusing Things to Do in Henley Beach

Swimming and Surfing: Henley Beach's crystal-clear, blue seas beckon swimmers of all abilities, while its steady waves provide great surfing conditions. The beach provides the ideal environment, whether your goal is to catch a wave or just take a cool plunge.

Beach Volleyball: Henley Beach has some courts for beach volleyball, making it a great place for friends and family to play some friendly rivalry. Bring a ball and enjoy the game while taking in the lovely scenery; the courts are free to use.

Walking and Cycling: Both bikers and pedestrians will find the Henley Beach promenade to be a picturesque path. It stretches along the coast and provides breathtaking views of the sea, making it the ideal location for a leisurely bike ride or a walk at sunset.

Fishing: Anglers often visit the jetty at Henley Beach. The jetty is a terrific area to throw a line and maybe catch local species like whiting or squid, whether you're an expert fisherman or a novice.

Eating in Henley Beach

Henley Beach is well known for its exciting food scene, which has a wide variety of establishments from upscale restaurants to laid-back cafés. Visitors may savor delectable meals while taking in an unhindered view of the ocean when eating waterfront.

Seaside Restaurants: Savor the finest seafood at any of the several eateries that line the shore. These restaurants provide anything from delicious gourmet meals to fish and chips, all of which are caught nearby.

Cafés and Ice Cream Shops: Henley Beach offers a wide selection of cafés and ice cream shops for those seeking a sweet treat or a lighter bite. Savor a handmade gelato or a cup of artisan coffee while admiring the atmosphere along the ocean.

International Cuisine: Henley Beach has a range of international eating choices, reflecting Adelaide's global culture. Every taste may be satisfied, with options ranging from Thai to Italian.

Henley Beach: A Sunset Experience

The sunsets at Henley Beach are perhaps one of its most magnificent features. The sky turns into a vivid painting as the day comes to an end, reflecting shades of pink, orange, and purple off the surface of the water. A tranquil moment of beauty may be found while watching the sunset from the jetty, the beach, or a restaurant by the water. It's the ideal way to start the evening with a hint of romance or conclude the day in style.

Pack a picnic and eat it on the beach for a more private sunset viewing experience. There are many places to spread out a blanket and relax along the beach's vast coastline as the sun sets.

Photography: Henley Beach is a favored location for photographers because of the stunning scenery during golden hour. Take pictures of the breathtaking landscape to preserve the memories of your trip.

COASTAL WALKS AND CONSERVATION PARKS

Glenelg and Henley Beach, two of Adelaide's most popular beaches, are connected by this picturesque walk down the coast. This stroll, which is around ten kilometers long and provides breathtaking views of the Gulf of St. Vincent, is ideal for people of all ages and fitness levels. Walkers may take in the calming sound of the waves, the lovely sea wind, and maybe even a cool plunge in the water along the route. Along the way are cafés and restaurants that invite you to stop and enjoy the local cuisine while seeing the coastline.

Walk at Hallett Cove Beach

Part of the Marino to Hallett Cove Conservation Park, the Hallett Cove Boardwalk is well-known for its breathtaking cliff-top vistas and geological importance. This strenuous trek, which is around 10.5 kilometers long and includes over 200 stairs as well as steep hills, is an enjoyable challenge for those who are more daring. The boardwalk is a gorgeous and instructive stroll that gives expansive views of the coastline and interpretive signs that explain the area's ancient geological history.

Adelaide's Conservation Parks

Park Morialta Conservation

Morialta Conservation Park is a hiking and wildlife lover's paradise, located just a short drive from Adelaide's central business district. The park offers a variety of walking paths that range in difficulty from simple to difficult, as well as rocky hills, gully landscapes, and seasonal waterfalls. A thorough tour of the park's features, including breathtaking views of the city and waterfalls, may be had on the Three Falls Grand Hike. Koalas, kangaroos, and several bird species may be seen at Morialta, making it an excellent place to see birds and other animals.

Park Cleland Conservation

Set in the stunning Adelaide Hills, Cleland Conservation Park provides a distinctive fusion of natural and interactive activities. Walking routes in the park run through thick vegetation and provide breathtaking views of Adelaide. The Cleland Animals Park, where guests may get up close and personal with Australian animals, such as kangaroos, wallabies, and koalas, is one of the park's attractions. Additionally, the park provides a chance to learn about conservation initiatives and the value of maintaining natural environments.

Park National Belair

Belair National Park, the oldest national park in South Australia, provides a diverse range of landscapes, animals, and history. Hikers, bikers, and even horseback riders may enjoy the park's vast network of paths, which wind through forests, lakes, and valleys. The State Flora Nursery and the Old Government House are two of the park's most famous features. In addition, the park has tennis courts, playgrounds, and picnic spots, making it an ideal family outing.

DAY TRIPS FROM ADELAIDE

KANGAROO ISLAND: WILDLIFE AND WILDERNESS

The journey starts with a charming drive from Adelaide to Cape Jervis, then a quick ferry trip over the Backstairs Passage to Penneshaw, the entry point to Kangaroo Island. The voyage itself is an integral part of the experience, with breathtaking vistas of the South Australian coastline and the opportunity to see dolphins breaching the wake of the ferry.

Discovering the Natural Wonders of the Island

Park Seal Bay Conservation

Seal Bay Conservation Park, one of the island's top attractions, provides guided excursions so visitors may see the critically endangered Australian sea lions in their native environment. Enjoying a unique and instructive wildlife experience, guests can get up close and personal with these amazing species as they lounge on the beach or play in the waves by strolling along boardwalks and sandy trails.

National Park of Flinders Chase

A visit to Flinders Chase National Park showcases the rocky beauty of Kangaroo Island's west end. The park is home to the well-known Admirals Arch and Remarkable Rocks, which are organic rock formations that have been shaped over millions of years by wind and waves and provide amazing picture ops. Nature lovers should not miss the park because of its extensive wildness, which is home to a wide variety of animals, including wallabies, echidnas, kangaroos, and other bird species.

The Wildlife Park at Kangaroo Island

The Kangaroo Island Animal Park provides an opportunity for anyone seeking a more interactive animal encounter to interact with kangaroos, wallabies, and even cradle a koala. Particularly in the wake of the 2019–2020 bushfires, the park is essential to the rescue and rehabilitation of animals and offers valuable information on island conservation initiatives.

Gourmet Treats and Regional Produce

Not only is Kangaroo Island visually stunning, but it also offers delectable food. Fresh fruit, such as Ligurian honey, fresh fish, and handcrafted cheeses, is abundant on the island due to its lush plains and uncontaminated waterways. Local farms, vineyards, and restaurants provide a sampling of the island's cuisine, providing a gourmet treat to go along with the natural excursion.

Getting the Most Out of a Day Outing

Even while a day excursion just scratches the surface of Kangaroo Island's amazing natural beauty and fauna, it provides a peek. It is advised to start early and carefully organize your schedule, concentrating on the main attractions to make the most of your time on the island and to completely enjoy the experience. There are guided excursions that provide easy navigation and enlightening details about the history, ecology, and conservation activities of the island.

An Appeal for Preservation

Seeing Kangaroo Island's natural splendor is just one aspect of the experience; another is realizing how crucial it is to protect these special places. Because of the fragility of the island's ecosystems, improper management of tourism might endanger its wildness and animals. Visitors may support local conservation programs, choose eco-friendly excursions.

ADELAIDE HILLS: HAHNDORF AND MOUNT LOFTY

With its strong German past, Hahndorf is a trip back in time rather than merely a place to visit. Visitors are welcomed by the sight of old buildings, artisan shops, and bakeries that fill the air with the perfume of freshly baked goodies as they stroll along the main street. The town displays the customs and architectural style of its German settlers, making it a living museum.

Cultural Exploration: With its museums, art galleries, and artisan stores, Hahndorf provides a distinctive cultural experience. The Hahndorf Academy is home to a craft store selling creations by South Australian artists, a collection of local artwork, and historical displays.

Culinary Highlights: The town is well known for its German food, which is served in traditional bakeries and pubs with real German-style lagers and specialty brews. Dishes like bratwurst, schnitzel, and pretzels are available. Hahndorf is a great site to try cool-climate wine varietals from the Adelaide Hills area, which are well-known for their pleasant temperatures.

Panoramic Views and Natural Magnificence at Mount Lofty

Mount Lofty Summit provides the most breathtaking panoramic views from Adelaide's downtown skyline to the seaside, and it's just a short drive from Hahndorf. At 710 meters above sea level, this viewpoint is well worth seeing.

Trekking to the Summit: The climb from Waterfall Gully to Mount Lofty Summit is a rewarding endeavor for people who want to get close to nature. The walk leads to the spectacular vistas at the summit after winding through beautiful bushland, past waterfalls, and among natural species.

Mount Lofty Botanic Garden: This vast garden, which is a celebration of cool-climate flora and has breathtaking displays of rhododendrons, magnolias, and camellias, is tucked away on the slopes of Mount Lofty. The garden's meandering walkways and secret ponds provide a tranquil haven that's ideal for a stroll.

Maximizing Your Day Trip Experience

Arrange Your Visit: Consider the season when planning your visit and get an early start to make the most of the

Adelaide Hills. While spring delivers blooms and a vivid green environment, autumn gives Hahndorf and the surrounding countryside a breathtaking display of changing leaves.

Transportation: Several tour companies provide day tours from Adelaide that include visits to Hahndorf, Mount Lofty, and other local landmarks. The Adelaide Hills are also readily accessible by vehicle.

Stay Longer: There is much more to discover in the Adelaide Hills, even if a day excursion just scratches the surface. Think about staying longer to take in more of the area's offerings, such as the several vineyards, the National Motor Museum in Birdwood, or Stirling's medieval town.

FLEURIEU PENINSULA: BEACHES, WINERIES AND WHALE WATCHING

Beaches: Surfing and Serenity

Some of South Australia's most picturesque beaches may be found scattered around the Peninsula's coastline. There is a stretch of sand for every kind of beach lover, from the family-friendly Christies Beach and Port Noarlunga, where placid waves allow leisurely swims, to the surfer's haven of Middleton.

Victor Harbor is yet another gem in the Peninsula's crown, featuring stunning beaches together with a quaint seaside town atmosphere. Reachable by causeway or the famous horse-drawn tram, Granite Island Recreation Park is an ideal location for a stroll with breathtaking views of the ocean.

Wineries: Showcasing the Finest in the Region

The McLaren Vale wine area, known for its quality wines, including Shiraz, Grenache, and Cabernet, is also located on the Fleurieu Peninsula. Nestled in this lovely setting are over 80 cellar doors, many of which provide gourmet dining experiences and tastings that highlight the region's agriculture.

For its cutting-edge wine experiences and avant-garde architecture, d'Arenberg Cube is a must-visit; Wirra Wirra Vineyards offers a more conventional but no less remarkable tasting experience. In addition to wine, the area is well-known for its handcrafted distilleries and brewers, which have something to offer every palette.

Whale watching: Magnificent Marine Life

The Fleurieu Peninsula is one of the greatest locations in Australia to see Southern Right Whales between May and October as they move to the warmer waters off the coast to mate and give birth. There are great places to observe whales in Encounter Bay, especially in the villages of Victor Harbor, Port Elliot, and Middleton.

Before setting out to observe these magnificent animals from the beach or embarking on a guided boat excursion for a closer look, anybody interested in learning more about them may start their journey at the South Australian Whale Centre at Victor Harbor.

Maximizing Your Day Trip Experience

Make a Route Plan: Make a schedule for the day that includes a variety of activities, starting in Adelaide. The morning is perfect for hiking or beach trips, while the afternoon is good for vineyard tours and tastings. The greatest time to observe these gentle giants is at twilight when whale watching occurs.

Travel Tip: Renting a vehicle is the ideal method to explore the Fleurieu Peninsula at your leisure since it is a large region. Verify the opening hours of vineyards and other attractions since some could need reservations, particularly during the busiest periods of the year.

Local Food and Produce: A trip to the Peninsula wouldn't be complete without sampling the regional food. The area is a sensory extravaganza, offering everything from specialty cheeses and chocolates available at several farmers' markets to ocean-fresh seafood at Star of Greece overlooking Port Willunga Beach.

OUTDOOR ACTIVITIES AND ADVENTURES

CYCLING AND MOUNTAIN BIKING TRAILS

A network of shared-use pathways is available in Belair National Park for use by horseback riders, bikers, and walkers. Based in Belair National Park, Escapegoat Adventures offers day adventures, excellent coffees, snacks, and bike rentals at The Goat Shed. Cycling enthusiasts may take in breathtaking views of the Adelaide Hills and surrounding areas from the several fire trails and shared-use paths found at Cleland Conservation Park.

Wetlands of Laratinga and the Mount Barker Linear Trail Popular too is the Mount Barker Linear Trail, which circles the Laratinga Wetlands and beyond. The serene marshes close to Mount Barker are encircled by some paths and boardwalks that pass through a variety of natural plants. Named after some of the local wildlife are trails like "Sacred Ibis," "Rosella," and "Chestnut Teal." In addition, there are some "hides" for bird viewing, a space for picnics and barbecues, and eco-friendly restrooms. The pathways in the wetlands are connected to the award-winning seven-kilometer Mount Barker Linear Trail, which follows the local streamline from Laratinga Wetlands to Keith Stephenson Park.

Kidman Trail

The Kidman path connects Willunga on the Fleurieu Peninsula to Kapunda in the Clare Valley. It is a multipurpose horseback riding, cycling, and walking path that spans 225 kilometers of roadsides, peaceful farm routes, woodland trails, and unmade road reserves. From Kuitpo Forest in the south, it meanders across the Adelaide Hills, passing through Echunga, Macclesfield, Balhannah, Woodside, Charleston, and Mount Torrens before joining the Barossa. The Kidman Trail is a picturesque, secure, and sustainable path that showcases the Mount Lofty Ranges' natural beauty, cultural heritage, and important sites. It makes use of already-existing paths and trails that pass through unmade road reserves, forest reserves, and other publicly accessible areas. Trail markers are used to indicate the route. The route has the honorary name Sir Sidney

Kidman, a well-known pastoralist and horse breeder from the area.

Trail of Tom Roberts

The Tom Roberts Horse Trail Network is intended for equestrian use, although it is also accessible to hikers and cyclists. This network of multipurpose trails over natural terrain essentially stretches from Cherry Gardens in the north to Kangarilla in the south and Woodcroft in the west. The network of trails, which was created by road verges, on-road connections, and unmade road reserves, includes Adelaide Hills destinations including Cherry Gardens, Coromandel East, Clarendon, Scott Creek, and Kangarilla.

Journey Across Australia Event

The Santos Tour Down Under, an annual cycling event conducted in January, is largely influenced by the difficult terrain of the Adelaide Hills. The world's top road cycling teams visit South Australia for this UCI World Tour event, which is the biggest cycling event in the Southern Hemisphere. Cycling aficionados line the course as spectators and participate in the public participation ride, making it very popular. Based at the renowned Uraidla Hotel, E-Go Bike Rentals provides touring e-bikes for rental and custom excursions year-round so you can take your time exploring the Central Adelaide Hills region.

WATERSPORTS: KAYAKING, SURFING AND FISHING

Torrens River Kayaking

In the heart of the city, the River Torrens provides an idyllic kayaking experience that's ideal for novices and those seeking a quiet trip. It's a great pastime for both adults and families because of the tranquil seas, which make navigating them simple. While kayaking along the river, you'll be able to take in the stunning scenery of the city, the verdant riverbanks, and maybe even some local animals.

Kayaking on Garden Island

Kayaking through ship graveyards and mangrove forests is an option on Garden Island, which is reachable from Port Adelaide, for those seeking a little more excitement. This region offers a distinct environment that is fascinating to explore. It is rich in marine life and wildlife and combines historical fascination with natural beauty.

Surfing: Take It All in

Known for its reliable waves, Middleton Beach, on the Fleurieu Peninsula, is a preferred location for surfers of all abilities. The beach provides more difficult breakers for skilled surfers as well as conditions that are perfect for novices wishing to learn. There are surf schools and rental businesses that provide instruction and equipment to anyone who is eager to learn how to surf or who wants to improve their abilities.

Moana Beach

Moana Beach, another jewel in Adelaide's surfing scene, offers surfers a welcoming and safe environment with its sandy bottom and clean seas. The beach has a more relaxed atmosphere and is less congested than other well-known locations, making it ideal for a day spent surfing. Additionally, cars are permitted on the beach at Moana, which makes it simple to carry your surf gear down to the water's edge.

Cast a line into abundance while fishing

River Port

Some of the greatest fishing locations are found near the city along the Port River. Anglers may anticipate catching a range of species here, such as bream, mullet, and sometimes even dolphins. Together with the extra benefit of being close to city facilities, the river's jetties and peaceful banks provide ideal locations for a leisurely day of fishing.

St. Vincent Gulf

If you're willing to go a little further, the enormous seas of the Gulf of St. Vincent are home to squid, whiting, and snapper, which makes it an excellent place for beach and boat fishing. Due to the gulf's large size, there are many undiscovered areas and reefs to discover, providing both the quiet of being out on the open sea and the excitement of a huge catch.

Maximizing Adelaide's Water Sports Opportunities

Following safety precautions and being mindful of the environment are essential for enjoying water sports in Adelaide to the fullest. Before leaving, always check the weather and sea conditions, put on the proper safety gear, and keep an eye out for marine life and protected areas. Numerous local companies provide guided tours and equipment rentals, making it simple to get the tools and expertise you need to improve your experience.

ARTS, CULTURE AND EVENTS

FESTIVALS AND EVENTS

Tarnanthi Festival

The rich and dynamic realm of Aboriginal and Torres Strait Islander art is celebrated at Tarnanthi. The festival provides a distinctive perspective on Australia's rich First Nations cultures by using the narrative potential of both traditional and contemporary art forms.

Adelaide Fringe

Fringe changes Adelaide and the rest of South Australia for six enchanting weeks in the summer. The festival features a wide range of colorful activities, including cabaret, theater, comedy, circus, music, visual arts, workshops, and much more, and it extends from Whyalla down to Mount Gambier.

Adelaide Festival

The Adelaide Festival, an event of really enormous proportions that delights audiences now and encourages future generations, is bold and exciting. In addition to showcasing some of the best firms and artists in the globe, AF commissions and supports the most avant-garde new work coming out of Australia.

WOMADelaide

WOMADelaide turns the verdant Botanic Park into a sovereign nation honoring both traditional and modern dance, art, and music. Along with seminars and speeches, street theater, cuisine demos, and a strong emphasis on sustainability, this joyful outdoor festival also includes other activities.

The History Festival in South Australia

The History Festival in South Australia is a yearly celebration of the state's rich and varied past. The History Festival, which takes place in May, examines the settings, narratives, artifacts, and concepts that shape who we are.

LIVE MUSIC AND NIGHTLIFE

The metropolis warms up as the sun sets. No matter whether you choose to party on a rooftop bar or get down on the dance floor, Adelaide's nightlife will keep you entertained all evening. Experience Adelaide's nightlife in a variety of enjoyable ways thanks to the city's bustling laneways and major streets, which are lined with live music venues and boutique pubs.

Adelaide's live music scene

Because of our passion for music, Adelaide became the first Australian city to be named a UNESCO City of Music in 2015. The distinction is a recognition of the city's music culture's depth, breadth, and vitality as well as its history, ambitions, worldwide reach, and legacy.

Where can I catch live music?

Adelaide has a diverse range of musical events, performances, and festivals. Around 80 live music venues around the city provide something to suit every mood, every night of the week.

Let there be rock

Intimate spaces like Jive, Ancient World, and Broadcast Bar are among the greatest spots to catch up-and-coming bands; for more well-known acts, visit bigger venues like Lion Arts Factory, Hindley Street Music Hall, or UniBar Adelaide. Places like Sugar, Electric Circus, Divide Nightclub, Rocket Bar and Rooftop, and so forth provide electronic music. Please be advised that many of these locations need you to be above 18.

The city is also home to a thriving bar and hotel culture, where several establishments showcase acoustic sessions and live bands. Try The Exeter Hotel, The Hotel Metropolitan (known to locals as The Metro), The Grace Emily, or Crown and Anchor. In North Adelaide, there's also The Lion Hotel and Royal Oak Hotel.

On a classical note

There is a wide variety of classical music available in Adelaide. The Adelaide Symphony Orchestra (ASO), which was founded in 1936, presents a colorful and varied repertoire all year long. They also serve as the orchestral backing for Adelaide Chamber Singers, Adelaide Youth Orchestra, and South Australia's State Opera.

The magnificent Adelaide Town Hall, the Nexus Multicultural Arts Centre, and the recognizable Elder Hall are the ideal places to view these shows.

BARS

Adelaide's bar culture is growing since the city is surrounded by world-class vineyards as well as artisanal beer and spirit makers. There is a bar close by that is perfect for you, whether you want to watch sports, have a celebration beverage, go bar hopping with your friends, or simply have a quiet drink. Adelaide bars

Adelaide's bar culture is growing since the city is surrounded by world-class vineyards as well as artisanal beer and spirit makers. There is a bar close by that is perfect for you, whether you want to watch sports, have a celebration beverage, go bar hopping with your friends, or simply have a quiet drink.

Adelaide bars

Adelaide's bar culture is growing since the city is surrounded by world-class vineyards as well as artisanal beer and spirit makers. There is a bar close by that is perfect for you, whether you want to watch sports, have a celebration beverage, go bar hopping with your friends, or simply have a quiet drink.

SHOPPING AND SOUVENIRS

LOCAL ARTISAN AND BOUTIQUES

The Hamper Specialist

A well-known Adelaide-based business, The Gift Specialist specializes in exquisite and superior gift baskets and hampers. Their suppliers are South Australian businesses who take great satisfaction in making sure all of their items are of the highest quality. Because of this, The Gifts Specialist is a great option for anybody searching for a special and opulent present.

Australia's 150 Unley Road, Unley, SA 5061

Little Love Co. Florist

Little Love Co. is a florist offering an incredible selection of plants, arrangements, and other trinkets (like bath salts!). For orders submitted before midnight on Monday through Saturday, they provide same-day delivery.

Australia's Norwood, SA 5067, 33 Kensington Road

Better Baskets in Adelaide

Adelaide Better Baskets is a gift basket retailer that focuses on providing affordable baskets to customers who want to give them as presents. They provide a large selection of foods and their baskets are excellent for individuals of all ages.

The Antique Market at Oldfield

Antique furniture is the specialty of Oldfield's Antique Market. The furniture is all antique and comes from many eras. A few of the items date back to the 1700s or even before. If you're interested in antiques, the shop is certainly worth checking out since it offers a lot of different things!

Australia's 1-9 Woolnough Road, Semaphore SA 5019

Have You Met Charlie

This unique gift store offers unique items from all around the globe that are quirky and out of the ordinary. It's the ideal place to discover the ideal gift for everyone because of the large selection of merchandise. In addition, its laneway setting makes it a fun stop for any visiting visitor.

Adelaide Arcade, Grenfell Street 12/118, Adelaide, Australia 5000

PRACTICAL INFORMATION

SAFETY AND EMERGENCY SERVICES

General Safety in Adelaide

Adelaide is generally considered a safe city for tourists and residents alike. The city prides itself on its welcoming atmosphere and low crime rate compared to other major cities. However, as in any urban area, it's advisable to take standard safety precautions:

- Avoid walking alone at night in poorly lit or less populated areas.

- Use licensed taxi services or reputable ride-sharing apps, particularly late at night.

Emergency Services

Emergency Number: In Australia, the number to call for police, fire, or ambulance in an emergency is **000**. This call is free of charge, and the service operates 24/7. When calling, be ready to provide your location, the nature of the emergency, and any other relevant details.

Non-Emergency Situations: For non-urgent police assistance, dial 131 444. If you need medical advice that's not life-threatening, the healthdirect hotline 1800 022 222 offers access to registered nurses 24/7.

Health Services

Adelaide boasts a comprehensive healthcare system, with numerous hospitals and clinics throughout the city. For tourists, it's important to have appropriate travel insurance to cover any potential medical costs. In case of medical needs, the **Royal Adelaide Hospital** is the largest in the city, equipped to handle a wide range of medical situations, including emergencies.

Beach Safety

Adelaide's beaches are beautiful, but it's crucial to swim safely:

- Always swim between the red and yellow flags, which indicate the area is patrolled by lifeguards.

- Be aware of and understand the signs of rips and currents, which can be dangerous even for experienced swimmers.

- If in doubt, ask a lifeguard for advice on swimming conditions.

Fire Safety

During the summer months, Adelaide and the surrounding regions can be prone to bushfires. If you're visiting rural areas or national parks, it's important to:

- Check the fire danger rating and any fire bans in place.

- Follow all guidelines and restrictions, especially regarding open flames.

- Be aware of and prepared to follow bushfire survival plans if you're staying in high-risk areas.

Wildlife and Outdoor Safety

Exploring Adelaide's natural landscapes and wildlife is a highlight for many visitors. To enjoy these experiences safely:

- Keep a safe distance from wild animals, including kangaroos and koalas. Feeding or attempting to touch them can be dangerous and is discouraged.

- When hiking or visiting conservation parks, inform someone of your plans, stay on marked trails, and carry sufficient water and sun protection.

Local Support Services

For tourists needing assistance, the South Australia Police offers a Tourist Police Unit, and the Adelaide

Visitor Information Centre can provide guidance and support for various inquiries, including safety advice and emergency services information.

CURRENCY AND BANKING

Currency

The official currency of Australia is the Australian Dollar (AUD), symbolized as $ or A$. It comes in denominations of 5, 10, 20, 50, and 100 dollar notes, as well as coins of 5, 10, 20, and 50 cents, and 1 and 2 dollar coins. Understanding the local currency is crucial for all transactions, from dining out to shopping and paying for services.

Banking

Adelaide boasts a robust banking network with branches of national and international banks readily accessible across the city. Major Australian banks include the Commonwealth Bank of Australia, Westpac, ANZ (Australia and New Zealand Banking Group), and NAB (National Australia Bank). These banks offer a range of services, including savings accounts, credit and debit cards, foreign currency exchange, and more. Most banks are open from Monday to Friday, typically between 9:30 am and 4:00 pm, with some branches offering extended hours on Thursdays or Saturdays.

ATMs: Automated Teller Machines (ATMs) are widely available throughout Adelaide, including in shopping centers, convenience stores, and on main streets. They accept major international debit and credit cards, although fees may apply for transactions, especially from international accounts.

Currency Exchange

For visitors, currency can be exchanged at the airport, banks, and designated currency exchange offices located in the city center and popular tourist areas. While exchanging money at the airport is convenient, better exchange rates are often found in the city. Always check the current exchange rate and inquire about commissions or fees before completing a transaction.

Using Credit and Debit Cards

Credit and debit cards are widely accepted in Adelaide, including Visa, MasterCard, and American Express. Contactless payments are also common for small transactions, offering a quick and convenient way to pay. When using an international card, be aware of potential transaction fees and currency conversion charges applied by your bank.

Tipping and Gratuity

In Australia, tipping is not as customary as in some other countries. Service charges are generally included in the bill in restaurants and cafes, and while tipping for exceptional service is appreciated, it is not expected. In bars, tipping is uncommon, and for taxis, rounding up the fare to the nearest dollar is a common way to offer a tip.

ITINERARIES AND PLANNING

SUGGESTED ITINERARIES

3-Day Itinerary: Adelaide Highlights

Day 1: City Exploration

-Morning: Start your day with a visit to the Adelaide Central Market. Enjoy breakfast at one of the local cafes and explore the variety of fresh produce and gourmet foods.

- **Afternoon**: Walk to the nearby South Australian Museum and Art Gallery of South Australia on North Terrace. Spend your afternoon immersed in the rich cultural and artistic heritage of South Australia.

- **Evening**: Dine at one of Adelaide's renowned restaurants on Rundle Street in the East End, followed by a stroll or a drink in the vibrant area.

Day 2: Adelaide Hills and Hahndorf

- **Morning**: Drive or join a tour of the Adelaide Hills. Visit the Mount Lofty Summit for panoramic views of Adelaide.

-

Afternoon: Head to Hahndorf, Australia's oldest surviving German settlement. Enjoy lunch at a local German pub and explore the quaint shops and galleries.

- **Evening**: Return to Adelaide. Consider an evening walk along the River Torrens, taking in the city lights.

Day 3: Glenelg Beach

- **Morning to Afternoon:** Take the tram to Glenelg, a popular beach suburb. Enjoy the beach, explore the shops along Jetty Road, and have lunch at one of the seaside eateries.

- **Evening**: Enjoy dinner back in the city or at Glenelg. If staying in the city, the Adelaide Oval RoofClimb offers a unique nighttime perspective of Adelaide.

5-Day Itinerary: Adding Barossa Valley and Kangaroo Island

Follow the 3-day itinerary for the initial days, then add:

Day 4: Barossa Valley

- Day Trip: Spend a day in the Barossa Valley, one of Australia's oldest and most renowned wine regions. Join a wine-tasting tour to explore some of the 150 wineries and cellar doors.

Day 5: Kangaroo Island

Early Start: Take an early morning tour to Kangaroo Island (note: this usually requires a very early start and can be quite a long day). Explore the natural wonders of the island, including Remarkable Rocks, Admirals Arch, and Seal Bay. Witness the diverse wildlife, such as kangaroos, koalas, and echidnas, in their natural habitat.

7-Day Itinerary: The Full South Australian Experience

Continue with the 5-day itinerary and add:

Day 6: Fleurieu Peninsula

- **Morning** to Afternoon: Explore the Fleurieu Peninsula with a visit to Victor Harbor.

Enjoy whale watching (seasonal) or visit the South Australian Whale Centre.

- **Late Afternoon:** Visit McLaren Vale for an afternoon wine tasting.

- **Evening**: Return to Adelaide for dinner.

Day 7: Leisure and Local Culture

- **Morning**: Visit the Adelaide Botanic Garden and enjoy a leisurely breakfast at the café.

- **Afternoon**: Spend your afternoon exploring any areas of Adelaide you may have missed or wish to revisit. The

Adelaide Zoo, North Adelaide's boutiques, or the beaches of Semaphore and Henley are all great options.

- **Evening**: Conclude your trip with a special dinner at one of Adelaide's fine dining restaurants or enjoy a casual meal at the Adelaide Night Market if available.

TIPS FOR FAMILIES, COUPLES AND SOLO TRAVELERS.

For Families

1. **Accommodation**: Look for family-friendly hotels or apartments in the city center or beachfront properties in Glenelg. These locations are not only convenient but also close to attractions and dining options suitable for all ages.

2. **Activities**: Adelaide Zoo, home to over 2,500 animals, is a must-visit for families. The Adelaide Botanic Garden offers ample space for children to explore, and the nearby Bicentennial Conservatory is perfect for spotting exotic plants and birds. The Beachhouse in Glenelg provides year-round entertainment with its waterslides, bumper boats, and mini-golf.

3. **Dining**: Choose family-friendly dining venues, with menus catering to younger palates. The Adelaide Central Market is a great spot for families to explore a variety of foods. Many restaurants in the city and beachside suburbs offer children's menus and play areas.

115

4. **Transport**: Utilize Adelaide's free City Loop bus for easy navigation around the city. The tram service to Glenelg is also convenient and offers a scenic route perfect for keeping the little ones entertained.

For Couples

1. **Romantic** Stays: Opt for boutique hotels or cozy B&Bs in the Adelaide Hills or near the beaches of Henley and Glenelg for a romantic retreat. For something unique, consider a vineyard stay in the Barossa Valley or McLaren Vale.

2. **Experiences**: Enjoy a sunset stroll along the River Torrens, taking in the city lights. For an unforgettable experience, book a hot air balloon flight over the Barossa Valley at sunrise, followed by a champagne breakfast.

3. **Dining**: Adelaide is renowned for its culinary scene. Book a table at one of the city's fine dining restaurants or enjoy a more intimate setting at a hidden laneway bar. Wine-tasting tours in nearby regions offer a delightful day out.

4. **Relaxation**: Spend a day relaxing at one of the many day spas in Adelaide or the Adelaide Hills. Many offer couples' packages, including massages and treatments.

For Solo Travelers

1. **Accommodation**: Consider staying in hostels or boutique hotels in the CBD for socializing opportunities and easy access to attractions. Many offer shared spaces and organize events, perfect for meeting fellow travelers.

2. **Exploration**: Adelaide is a bike-friendly city with free bike hire available, making it easy to explore at your own pace. Joining guided tours, especially to wine regions or Kangaroo Island, can also enhance your solo travel experience.

3. **Safety**: Adelaide is generally safe for solo travelers. Still, it's wise to stay aware of your surroundings, especially at night. Keep valuables secure and let someone know of your travel plans, particularly if venturing into remote areas.

4. **Networking**: Check out local meetups or events tailored to your interests. Adelaide has a vibrant arts scene, with festivals and exhibitions that offer great opportunities to connect with locals and other travelers.

General Tips for All Travelers

- **Seasons**: Plan your visit according to the season. Summers are great for beaches, while spring and autumn offer comfortable weather for exploring the wine regions and natural attractions.

- **Connectivity**: Take advantage of free Wi-Fi spots in the city, including libraries, cafes, and public spaces, to stay connected.

- **Local Produce:** Don't miss out on South Australia's local produce. Visit farmers' markets and local eateries to taste the region's best.

CONCLUSION

In the pages of this Adelaide travel guide, we embarked on an extraordinary journey through a city that captivates the heart and soul. Our adventure was filled with moments of awe and inspiration, leaving an indelible mark on our memories.

We ventured through the bustling streets of Adelaide, discovering its vibrant culture, rich history, and culinary delights. We explored the natural wonders of the Adelaide Hills and the pristine beaches of Glenelg. Our taste buds danced at the Adelaide Central Market, and our hearts swelled with the melodies of the city's festivals.

Yet, amidst the beauty of the landscapes and the flavors of the cuisine, it was the warmth of the people that truly touched our hearts. The welcoming smiles of locals and the shared stories with fellow travelers forged emotional connections that transcended borders.

Unforgettable moments unfolded before our eyes - the sunrise over the Barossa Valley vineyards, the laughter of children playing on Glenelg Beach, and the kaleidoscope of colors at the Adelaide Fringe Festival. These moments are etched in our souls, reminding us of the beauty of this world.

As you continue your exploration of Adelaide, remember these practical tips: embrace the seasons, savor the local produce, and immerse yourself in the city's vibrant events. Adelaide's magic lies in its diversity, and there's always something new to discover.

I extend my heartfelt gratitude to the people of Adelaide, who welcomed us with open arms, and to you, dear reader, for allowing me to be your guide on this remarkable journey.

As our adventure in Adelaide comes to an end, I encourage you to keep exploring, discovering, and embracing the beauty of the world around you. Travel is not just about places; it's about the connections we make and the stories we share.

With wanderlust in our hearts and a world waiting to be explored, I bid you farewell until our paths cross again.

Warmest wishes,
Mabel Martin

Printed in Great Britain
by Amazon

42933608R00069